MW00816980

SCRIPTURE

ILLUMINATED

SCRIPTURE ILLUMINATED

A Coloring Book for Prayer and Meditation

Art by Estelle Chandelier

Introduction by Emmanuelle Rémond-Dalyac

Pauline
BOOKS & MEDIA

Boston

ISBN 10: 0-8198-9074-X

ISBN 13: 978-0-8198-9074-0

Originally published in French as *Paix Intérieure, 72 paroles de la Bible Enluminures à colorier* © by Yves Briend Éditeur / Salvator, Paris, 2015, Propriétaire Yves Briend Éditeur S.A.

Art by Estelle Chandelier

Scripture texts from the book of Psalms are taken from *The Psalms: A Translation from the Hebrew*, translated by Miguel Miguens, copyright © 1995, Daughters of St. Paul. All rights reserved. Used with permission.

Other Scripture quotations contained herein are from the *New Revised Standard Version Bible: Catholic Edition,* copyright © 1989, 1993, Division of Christian Education of the National Council of the Churches of Christ in the United States of America. Used by permission. All rights reserved.

"P" and PAULINE are registered trademarks of the Daughters of St. Paul.

All rights reserved. No part of this book may be reproduced or transmitted in any form or by any means, electronic or mechanical, including photocopying, recording, or by any information storage and retrieval system, without permission in writing from the publisher.

Edition and translation copyright © 2017, Daughters of St. Paul

Published by Pauline Books & Media, 50 Saint Paul's Avenue, Boston, MA 02130-3491

Printed in Korea

www.pauline.org

Pauline Books & Media is the publishing house of the Daughters of St. Paul, an international congregation of women religious serving the Church with the communications media.

1 2 3 4 5 6 7 8 9   21 20 19 18 17

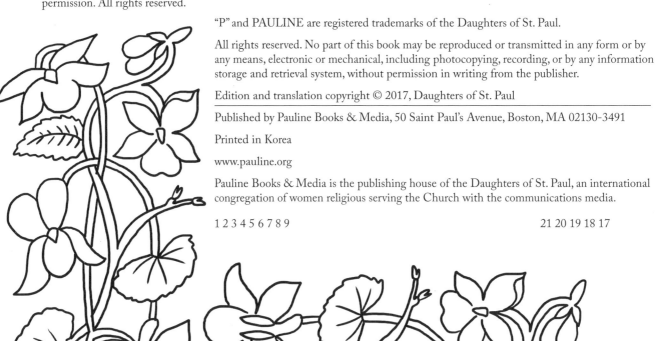

"The word is very near
to you; it is in your
mouth and in your heart
for you to observe."

DEUTERONOMY 30:14

The Art of Illumination

In admiring an illuminated manuscript, who has not thought of the monks in the scriptorium of their monasteries, leaning on their manuscripts with pen in hand, copying the Gospel and other biblical texts for the greater glory of God and the edification of the faithful? The art of illumination, however, is not found only in medieval Christianity. In ancient Egypt, rolls of papyrus were illustrated in the time of the New Kingdom (c. 1550–1077 BC). This technique spread throughout the Mediterranean after the conquest of Egypt by Alexander the Great (fourth century BC). But the papyrus was made from the stem of the papyrus plant, which did not allow for applying several layers of paint. Besides, it easily disintegrated due to the effect of humidity when it was exported to countries more temperate than Egypt.

The Book: A Technological Revolution

The art of illumination took off later, in the first century of our era, with the invention of the vellum or parchment codex. Made of pages that could turn instead of a scroll that would unroll, the codex was a technological revolution. Historians do not hesitate to compare it to printing in the way it changed people's reading habits. The scroll was held in two hands, with a panoramic vision of the text, which was in several columns. This made it necessary to read aloud continuously. The codex, instead, being easier to handle and browse through, made possible a more selective and silent reading. It could include more text because the text was written on both sides, and it was easy to add to the number of pages.

This great advantage explains why parchment was generally adopted despite the meticulous care required to produce it. Parchment was made from the skin of a calf or sheep soaked in a solution of water and lime [calcium hydroxide], and then beaten out and stretched. (The term "vellum" was reserved for the skin of a stillborn calf, rare and prized.) After being dried, the skin was polished with a pumice stone, the vellum was folded in two, four, or eight, according to the dimensions of the book. Then the pages were sewn. A book of sixteen sheets in a small format required fifteen skins. The work of making parchment took a long time!

When the codex was ready, the copyist took over: he would adjust the upper sheet of paper of the bundle and perforate all the pages with the help of a hole punch. He would then draw lines between the perforations for spacing, so that the margins would be the same for each page. The illuminator, who was not the copyist, would show him the space that had to be reserved for the ornamental borders, the letters and the miniatures, the name given to the figurative scenes that sometimes took up the whole page. The copyist would use ink made with charcoal, and the illuminator would use a paintbrush to apply colors made from animal, vegetable, or mineral sources, mixed with some egg whites or honey. With this method, all sorts of texts were illuminated in antiquity: poems; treatises on the natural sciences, in particular on flowers; plays, etc. This art was elevated to the rank of the major arts around the fourth century, when Christianity became the official religion of the Roman Empire.

The Illuminated Bible

The Desert Fathers, the first Christian hermits in Egypt during the third century, had already used the art of calligraphy for the Bible in their huts. In the West, this art disappeared with the collapse of the Roman Empire. The upheavals of war made it difficult to practice this art that requires concentration, calm, and silence. But new developments occurred with the rise of Irish monasticism, under the guidance of Saint Columban. In the sixth century he sent missionaries to Scotland. The most famous example of their work is the illuminated Gospel book from the monastery at Lindisfarne, which dates from around the year 698.

The practice of illuminating the Bible expressed devotion and honor for the sacred character of the text, but it also had a practical function: the Book of the Gospels that arranged the Gospels in their liturgical order also contained visual indications that allowed one to identify the context of the text before the reading began. And during a time in which these texts were always proclaimed in Latin, the gospel scenes could also be viewed from afar by the assembly of the faithful. The missionaries carried these texts with them all across Europe. The beauty of the written text, enhanced by the beautiful images, made for a powerful form of evangelization.

The books were rare because producing them was a long and costly process, so their possessors enjoyed great social prestige. Emperors, kings, and princes collected them, and during the twelfth century, when European cities developed, rich merchants wanted them too. The illuminators left the quiet of the monasteries and spread to the new universities of Europe, such as Paris or Oxford. Their style continued to develop over the centuries.

Gutenberg's invention of printing in 1450 retained for a time some illumination at the heads of chapters and on borders, but illumination as a major art was gradually lost with the development of engraving and the mastery of full-color printing. In our imagination, illumination is henceforth associated, like the cathedrals of the cities or the abbeys of the countryside, with the time of the Middle Ages and its marvels of a Christian civilization.

A Thousand Years of Creative Art

The Celtic Style

This style was developed in Ireland under the impetus of the monks of Saint Columban and is marked by a mixture of interlaced spirals and geometric designs in the page borders. The Celtic style of illumination principally used solid shades of red and green with red dotted lines applied around the initial letter of the page to soften its contour.

This style of art can be found on pages 16–17, 18–19, 26–27, 72–73.

The late Celtic style includes more exotic themes using designs based on animals: the animals are twisted to adapt to the form of the letters.

This style of art can be found on pages 44–45, 66–67.

The Roman Style

This style spread in Europe at the beginning of the ninth century after the Court of Charlemagne linked the Roman world with that of Northern Germany. After his crowning at Rome, the new emperor commanded his copyists to add Mediterranean motifs to their Gospel books: palm leaves and branches, acanthus leaves, multicolor gradations. They often had historiated initials, which were letters that contained small scenes of something narrated in the text.

This style of art can be found on pages 32–33, 46–47, 56–57.

The Gothic Style

This style developed in the cities of France and England, where lay people, rather than monks, began illuminating manuscripts. They most often decorated books of hours and liturgical psalters, containing a calendar and eight chapters of psalms, with hymns and prayers. The most famous of these is that of the Duke of Berry, produced in Paris between 1413 and 1416 by the Limbourg brothers. Decorated in gold, the borders are dotted with flowers and the pictures are executed in watercolors.

This style of art can be found on pages 24–25, 28–29, 58–59, 76–77.

The Renaissance Style

The art of illumination was also influenced by the Renaissance, which restored the ancient Greek and Latin heritage and spread in Europe, especially in Italy, in the fifteenth century. The style called the "white vine" style appeared, in which the initial letter was interlaced by a white climbing vine on a color base. This style adopted some Roman elements copied from monuments and tombs found in excavations.

This style of art can be found on pages 48–49.

A Few Tips

The Colors

Vary your selection of colors from one illumination to another. If you wish a softer effect, work with harmonious combinations of pastels using different shades that you develop on a scale of your own. For vivacity, choose primary colors (red, yellow, blue) or work with some combinations: red and green, blue and orange, yellow and violet. You can use models found on the cover or look for inspiration online.

Meditate, Pray

While coloring, the biblical citations can also become privileged moments of *lectio divina*, which is a prayerful reading of the Bible. Meditation can thus be serenely joined to the work of coloring. This is the balance we should strive for, according to the teaching of Saint Benedict, founder of many monastic communities in the sixth century. For example, you can proceed in the following way:

- Choose an appropriate time, when you are certain of not being disturbed. Give yourself enough time, at least twenty minutes.
- Choose a citation by consulting the index (pp. 78–79).
- Slowly read the text, paying attention to each word.
- Let the text resonate within you, with your own experience.
- Illuminate [or color] the words, beginning with those that speak to you.

As you work, open yourself if you can and spend some time in prayer, which is a time of dialogue with God. As Saint Augustine said, "Your prayer is your word addressed to God. When you read, it is God who is speaking to you; when you pray, it is you who are speaking with God."

When the Word of God suddenly opens up an interior silence in which God makes himself present, focus your attention on this as you open yourself to this time of contemplation.

As a DEER thirsts for streams of water

so, my God,
does my soul
pant for you.
Athirst is my soul
for God, for
the living God;
"When shall
I go and see
God's face?"

PSALM 42:2–3

The **V**OICE

of my beloved!

Look, he comes,
leaping upon the
mountains,
bounding over the
hills.

SONG OF SOLOMON 2:8

Trust in the LORD
WITH ALL YOUR

EART

and do not rely
on your own
insight.
In all your ways
acknowledge him,
and he will make
straight your
paths.

PROVERBS 3:5–6

TGive
HANKS
to the
LORD

for he is good,
for his loving kindness
is forever.

PSALM 107:1

Listen!

I am standing at the door,
knocking;

if you hear my

VOICE
and open the door, I will
come in to you and eat
with you, and you with me.

Revelation 3:20

21

But while he was still far off, his

FATHER

saw him and

was filled with
compassion;
he ran and put his arms
around him and kissed him.

LUKE 15:20

23

LESS

the LORD, my soul;

and all that is in me
bless his holy name. . . .
He is compassionate
and gracious,
patient in the face of
provocation, and rich in
loving kindness.

PSALM 103:1, 8

Draw near to
GOD,
and he will

DRAW

near to you.

JAMES 4:8

I have been
crucified with

CHRIST,

and it is no longer

who live,
but it is
CHRIST
who lives in me.

GALATIANS 2:19–20

29

The Lord, your God,
is in your midst,
a warrior who gives victory;
he will rejoice over you
with gladness,
he will

BENEW
you in
his love;
he will exult over you
with loud singing . . .

ZEPHANIAH 3:17

31

"For God so loved the world that he gave his **O**NLY SON

so that
everyone who
believes
in him may not
perish but may
have eternal
life."

"PEACE

I leave with you; my peace
I give to you. I do not give
to you as the world gives.

Do not let your hearts
be troubled, and do not let
them be afraid."

JOHN 14:27

I want their hearts to be

encouraged

and

NITED

in love, so that they
may have all the riches
of assured understanding
and have the knowledge of
God's mystery, that is,
Christ himself. . . .

COLOSSIANS 2:2

For this reason I bow my knees before the Father, from whom

every family in heaven and on EARTH

takes its name. I pray that,
according to the riches
of his glory, he may grant that
you may be strengthened
in your inner being . . .

EPHESIANS 3:14–16

Love is

ATIENT. . . .

It does not insist on its own way; it is not irritable or resentful; it does not rejoice in wrongdoing, but rejoices in the truth. It bears all things, believes all things, hopes all things, endures all things. Love never ends.

1 Corinthians 13:4–8

"ASK,

and it will be given you;
search, and you will find;
knock, and the door will be
opened for you."

MATTHEW 7:7

If a shepherd has

a hundred
SHEEP,
and one of
them has
gone astray,

does he not leave the ninety-nine on the mountains and go in search of the one that went astray? And if he finds it, truly I tell you, he rejoices over it more than over the ninety-nine that never went astray.

MATTHEW 18:12–13

And

MARY said,

"My soul magnifies the Lord,
and my spirit rejoices in God
my Savior,
for he has looked with favor
on the lowliness of his servant."

LUKE 1:46–48

So God created
humankind
in his

IMAGE,

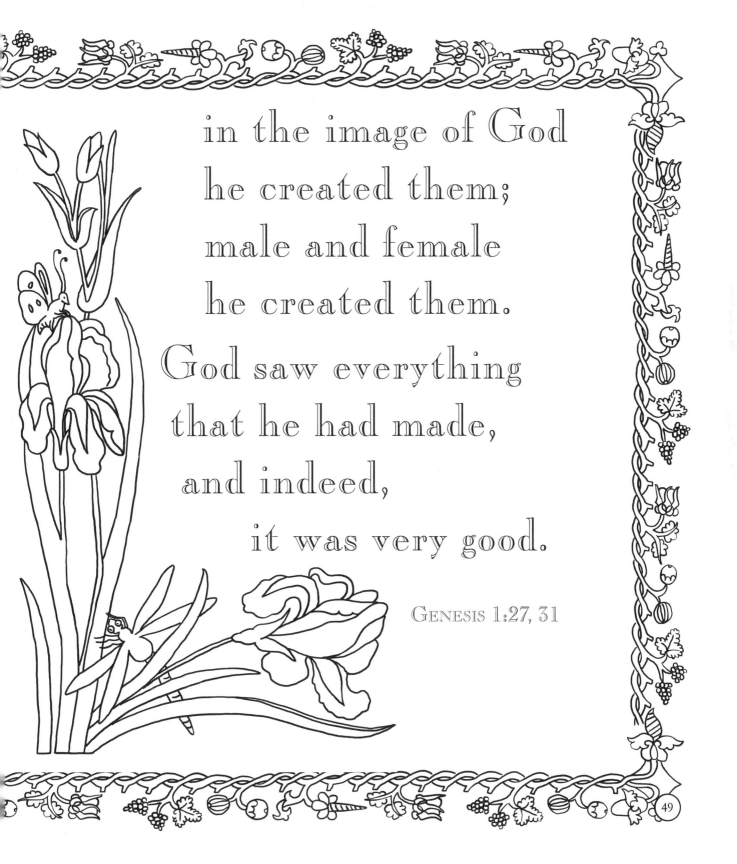

in the image of God
he created them;
male and female
he created them.
God saw everything
that he had made,
and indeed,
it was very good.

GENESIS 1:27, 31

I led them with cords
of human kindness,
with

BANDS
of love.

I was to them like those
who lift infants to their
cheeks.
I bent down to them
and fed them.

HOSEA 11:4

"Let the
ITTLE
children
come
to me;

do not stop them; for it is to such as these that the kingdom of God belongs. Truly I tell you, whoever does not receive the kingdom of God as a little child will never enter it."

"No one can come to me unless drawn

F by the ATHER

who sent me;
and I will raise
that person up
on the last day."

JOHN 6:44

"COME

to me, all you that are weary and are carrying heavy burdens, and I will give you rest. Take my yoke upon you, and learn from me; for I am gentle and humble in heart, and you will find rest for your souls. For my yoke is easy, and my burden is light."

Humble yourselves . . . under the mighty

Band

of God, so that he may
exalt you in due time.
Cast all your anxiety
on him, because he
cares for you.

1 PETER 5:6–7

But God proves
his love for us in that
while we still
were sinners

CHRIST died for us.

ROMANS 5:8

Be gracious to me,
O God,
as befits

OUR

loving kindness.
In the great tenderness
of your love, wipe out
my transgressions.

PSALM 51:3

GOD

is love, and those who abide in love abide in God, and God abides in them.

1 JOHN 4:16

. . . neither death, nor life, nor angels, nor rulers, nor things present, nor things to come, nor powers, nor height, nor depth, nor anything else in all creation,

will be able
to separate us
from the love
of God
in Christ

JESUS

our Lord.

ROMANS 8:38–39

The steadfast love
of the LORD

EVER

ceases,

his mercies never
come to an end;
they are new every morning;
great is your faithfulness.

LAMENTATIONS 3:22–23

Yet even now, says the LORD,
return to me with all your
heart,
with fasting, with weeping, and
with mourning;
rend your hearts and not your
clothing.

RETURN to the LORD, your God, for he is gracious and merciful, slow to anger, and abounding in steadfast love . . .

JOEL 2:12–13

I have called you by name,
you are mine . . .
you are precious in my sight,
and honored,

AND I

LOVE

You. . .

Isaiah 43:1, 4

73

the Father has loved me,
so I have loved you;
abide in my love.
If you keep my
commandments,
you will abide in
my love. . . . "

"I have told you this so that my joy may be in you and your

J OY

may be complete."

John 15:11

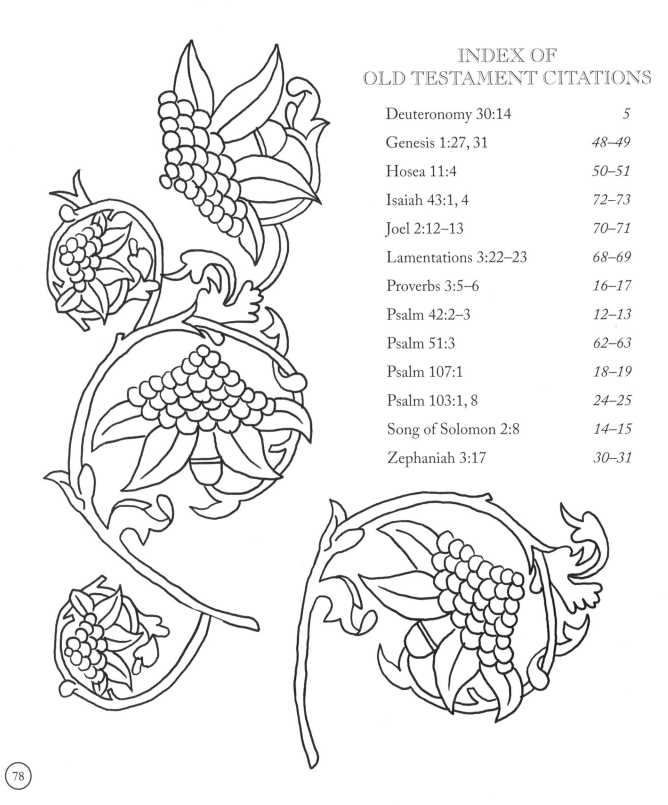

INDEX OF OLD TESTAMENT CITATIONS

INDEX OF
NEW TESTAMENT CITATIONS

Pauline
BOOKS & MEDIA

The Daughters of St. Paul operate book and media centers
at the following addresses. Visit, call, or write the one nearest you today,
or find us at www.paulinestore.org

CALIFORNIA
3908 Sepulveda Blvd, Culver City, CA 90230   310-397-8676
3250 Middlefield Road, Menlo Park, CA 94025   650-369-4230

FLORIDA
145 S.W. 107th Avenue, Miami, FL 33174   305-559-6715

HAWAII
1143 Bishop Street, Honolulu, HI 96813   808-521-2731

ILLINOIS
172 North Michigan Avenue, Chicago, IL 60601   312-346-4228

LOUISIANA
4403 Veterans Memorial Blvd, Metairie, LA 70006   504-887-7631

MASSACHUSETTS
885 Providence Hwy, Dedham, MA 02026   781-326-5385

MISSOURI
9804 Watson Road, St. Louis, MO 63126   314-965-3512

NEW YORK
64 W. 38th Street, New York, NY 10018   212-754-1110

SOUTH CAROLINA
243 King Street, Charleston, SC 29401   843-577-0175

TEXAS
Currently no book center; for parish exhibits or outreach evangelization,
contact: 210-569-0500, or SanAntonio@paulinemedia.com, or P.O. Box
761416, San Antonio, TX 78245

VIRGINIA
1025 King Street, Alexandria, VA 22314   703-549-3806

CANADA
3022 Dufferin Street, Toronto, ON M6B 3T5   416-781-9131